A031024424

D1809133

VOLVO

by

John Creighton

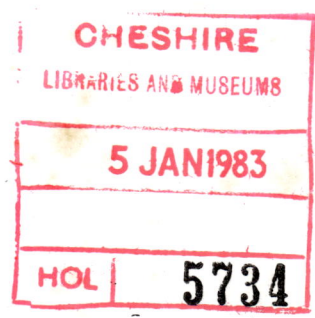
IAN HENRY PUBLICATIONS
1982

ISBN 0 86025-838-6

Made and Printed in Great Britain by
Robert Hartnoll Ltd. Bodmin, Cornwall
for Ian Henry Publications Ltd.
38 Parkstone Avenue, Hornchurch, Essex RM11 3LW

The name Volvo is synonymous with reliability, strength, precision engineering and safety, these properties all being integral features of the vast range of Volvo products, from cars to buses, tractors to trucks. The top five markets for car sales are Sweden, Great Britain, U.S.A., West Germany and the Netherlands and Volvo Car Division accounts for just over half of corporate sales, with Car Divisions in Gothenburg and Eindhoven (Netherlands) responsible for the manufacture, marketing and development of Volvo's car programme. There are over thirty thousand people engaged in car production with outlets for cars in about a hundred countries and, although production of the 240/260 series is based in Sweden, assembly takes place in several countries, the biggest assembly plants outside Sweden being found in Holland and Belgium,

with others in Malaysia, Canada Indonesia and Australia.

A modern technical centre in Gothenburg, opened in 1972, ensures that factors such as safety, reliability and comfort are fully examined, and a gruelling test area at Hällered is the scene for high speed tests and endurance, while mud and salt stretches are designed to test Volvo's famous rust-proofing protection.

Components such as transmission, engines, axles and interiors are manufactured in Volvo's own factories, but a sub-contractor scheme allows for a large number of parts to come from over one thousand alternative sources and so, for instance, Volvo, along with Peugeot and Renault, has an engine plant in France where the B27 engine is built, this unit powering the 260 series. The polemics surrounding discussions concerning the value of buying British cars in order to augment U.K. car sales should be carefully considered, since about one quarter of the average Volvo car's contents is British, and the Volvo procurement system in Britain is based at the port of Immingham from where all Volvo components leave for Sweden, as well as Volvo concerns in other lands, co-ordinated from the company's material control department in Birmingham.

From Volvo's inception in 1926, with a capital of 200,000 Swedish Kroner and its first products of the 'Jakob' car and the first truck a year later, the company has concentrated on safety and quality, not only for trucks and cars, but also for other products such as agricultural machinery, buses and jet engines, and establishments, such as those at Hällby, Trollhättan, Malmar and Skövde, contribute to achieving perfection in all Volvo's products. The history of the company demonstrates the expansion of Volvo, in 1930 share majority

in Penta plant at Skövde was acquired, followed by a series of mergers, whilst in the 60s the group expanded in places, such as Peru, where trucks and buses were assembled, in Canada and Belgium, where car assembly plants were established, and in Malaysia. During the 1970s significant moves included the acquisition of Ailsa trucks in Glasgow, co-operation opened with DAF of Holland, and an import and marketing company for Volvo in Japan was set up with the Japanese group, Teijin Ltd.

During 1981 Friedrich Jackson from Volvo was awarded the Safety Award for Engineering Excellence from the American traffic safety association, NHTSA, this recognition underlining the increasing international appeal of Volvo, further emphasised by the 1981 figures, which indicated the highest penetration ever made by the Volvo group in its 24-year history in the U.K.

An early OV4

THE EARLY DAYS

The year 1927 saw Charles Lindbergh fly solo from New York to Paris in the 'Spirit of St.Louis', while Al Jolson sang 'Sonny Boy' and Henry Ford decided to cease production of the T-Ford after building more than fifteen million of them. In Sweden a new car and a new company came into being as the first series-produced Volvo car came off the production line of a Gothenburg factory on 14th April, 1927.

This car was officially designated OV4, although its makers nicknamed it 'Jakob' — an elegant vehicle, being open in design with a frame of red beech and ash with metal panels. The main figures behind this magnificent vehicle were Gustaf Larson and Assar Gabrielson,

an engineer and an economist respectively, who had taken advantage of the relatively low wages paid in Sweden and the challenge of the Scandinavian climate, which necessitated a solid car. The men began work with their own capital, but the Swedish ball bearing company of SKF was so impressed with their plans and skills that it provided premises and financial support, and AB Volvo was born, the Latin word 'volvo' meaning 'I roll'.

The Swedish public was also a contributory factor to the new car in that increasing sales of cars augured well for a new model — in 1924 there were 46,000 cars and in 1927 81,000 — and so the two men had designed and sold a car whose durability and excellent quality would become the hall-mark of their business.

The new OV4 received power from a four cylinder engine

developing not less than 28h.p., and allowing the 'Jakob' model to attain a maximum speed of 60 k.p.h. Initial sales were not very encouraging since the open body was not ideal for the harsh Swedish weather, although the robust design made the vehicle an excellent choice for the rough roads. Larson and Gabrielson decided to make a covered version and some months later a second model, the PV4, appeared and, subsequently, sales improved.

By using the Jakob chassis and designing a covered version the company had introduced a popular car whose 'Pegamoid' finish of artifical leather gave the PV4 an expensive look. A further development of this type provided the public with a car whose luxuries included bumpers, and the box-like design of the PV4 reflected the trend of the 30s which favoured spacious cars driven by powerful six cylinder engines.

Assar Gabrielson and Gustaf Larson were quite pleased with progress made in the domestic Swedish market, but were always eager to promote their new vehicle abroad, so neighbouring Scandinavian countries of Finland, Norway and Denmark became importers of the car. This export drive was helped be advertising and an event in Russia in 1928, when the PV4 car was a competitor in the combined speed-economy-quality competition, whose route was Moscow to Leningrad and back to Moscow: the world then found out that the PV4 was a strong

OV4
Two PV4s

and reliable car, since it won its class and survived the arduous Russian roads and the cold temperatures.

Volvo trucks were based on the same chassis as the early cars and the name Volvo was thus associated with the new trucks that appeared during the late 1920s, which like the PV4, reflected excellent engineering and construction techniques.

PV651-652 and TR671-674

VOLVO CARS OF THE 1930s

Volvo's first six cylinder car had a top speed of 110 k.p.h. and featured hydraulic brakes and a synchronised gearbox allowing for comfort and safety factors: the PV651-652 and TR671-674 came on the market between 1929 and 1934, sporting the by-now-familiar diagonal line across the exterior of the radiator and a spare tyre attached to the running board.

PV655 employed as an ambulance

This range of cars proved popular for private owners and Volvo also manufactured one as a seven seater taxi, whose spacious interior and safety features made it a ready choice for cab drivers in Sweden.

The 1930s was a time when world events often included news of cars and their achievements and Volvo were determined to keep pace with modern developments; in 1929, for example, there were 148 different makes and variations of cars in Germany, 109 in France, and 70 or more in America, while 1930 saw the Englishman, Eyston, increase the world speed record for cars to 560 k.p.h.

Volvo, too, wanted a place in the fast-moving 30s and a niche in the expanding car market: consequently, they brought out a number of models to challenge the growing number of designs elsewhere in the world car market. The years 1933 to 1935 witnessed the

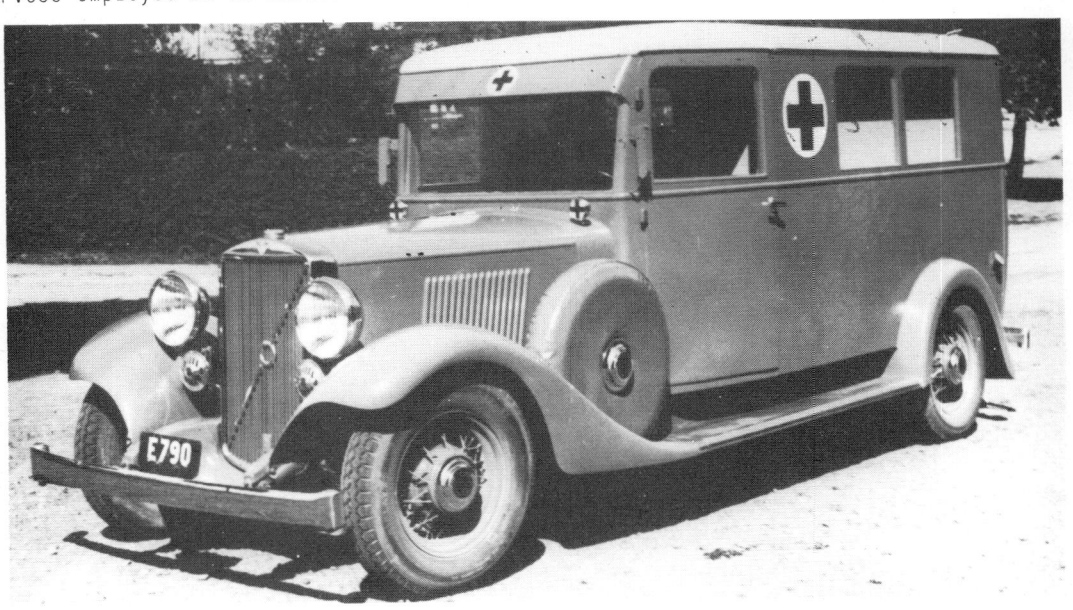

PV657 ambulance

Volvo luxury car, whose three speed gearbox and six cylinder engine of 3.27 litres made it a pleasure to drive; with bumpers as standard equipment and the enclosed spare wheel still on the running board, the PV653-654 and TR676-679 series were a force to be reckoned with

The box type style of car came to an end with Volvo's PV659, built between 1935 and 1938, whose new feature was the engine with an output of 80h.p. The PV658-659 range coincided with relevant world events in motor transport, as in 1936 Michelin of France introduced tyres with steel wires in their composition — forerunners of the modern steel braced radial tyres — and in 1938 Eyston was overtaken by Cobb in the land speed record with 595 k.p.h.

Volvo by the middle of the 1930s had an impressive range of cars — and its truck sales were also doing well, producing about 5,000 in 1940.

The summary of Volvo cars for the early 30s (opposite) may help to appreciate the many models.

During the second half of the 1930 period, Volvo had considerable success with the PV658-659 model and, by now, the good name of the company renowned for producing a sturdy and reliable car had encouraged taxi firms to buy newer designs in addition to taxis, such as the TR678 and TR679, made from 1934 to 1935. The Volvo TR701, 703 and 704 were equipped with a taxi body and during 1935-37 a total of almost 950 taxis in the TR70 series came on the market, each with an output of 80-84 b.h.p. and a six cylinder engine. The TR702 was not a popular make — in fact only eleven appeared — and, built

PV658-659

8

VOLVO CARS IN THE EARLY 1930s

Year of manufacture	Model	Number manufactured	Body type	Displacement c c	Number of cylinders	Output B.H.P.	Wheel base metres
1929-34	PV 650	206	Sep.frame	3,010	6	55	2.95
1929-32	PV 651)	2,176	Sedan	3,010	6	55	2.95
1929-33	PV 652)		Sedan	3,010	6	55	2.95
1930-34	TR 670	88	Sep.frame	3,010	6	55	3.10
1930-31	TR 671)	200	Taxi	3,010	6	55	3.10
1929-31	TR672)		Taxi	3,010	6	55	3.25
1932-34	TR 674	138	Taxi	3,010	6	55	3.25
1933-34	PV 653	230	Sedan	3,266	6	65	2.95
1933-34	PV 654	361	Sedan	3,266	6	65	2.95
1933-35	PV 655	62	Sep.frame	3,266	6	65	3.55
1934	TR 675	2	Sep.frame	3,266	6	65	3.10
1934-35	TR 676	29	Taxi	3,266	6	65	3.10
1934	TR 677	2	Sep.frame	3,266	6	65	3.25
1934-35	TR 678	39	Taxi	3,266	6	65	3.25
1934	TR 679	114	Taxi	3,266	6	65	3.25

on a separate body type, rather than the taxi body type, this vehicle had limited use.

Unlike the TR702, Volvo had tremendous success with their PV36, constructed between 1935 and 1938, whose six cylinder engine, displacement of 3,670cc and 2.95 metre wheel base, attracted the Swedish car buyer resulting in the manufacture of five hundred PV36 cars of separate frame design. Only one model was made with the sedan body in 1935 and was called PV36ch. It should be noted, however, that the PV36 or 'Carioca' was Volvo's first streamlined car and, for its time, was a modern vehicle which shared nothing of the accepted 'box' design found, not only in Sweden, but also in America during the 1930s. The comfort and visual appeal of the PV36 were its selling points, while the independent front suspension aided travel, but the high price for such luxuries restricted this model to affluent customers.

TR676-679

PV658-659: the last of the box-style
bodywork

'Carioca' or PV36

PV51

THE PV5 SERIES

The PV5 series contained a number of Volvo cars produced between 1936 and 1945 with the forerunner, PV51, coming on the market in 1936, proving to be a:n impressive and reliable car with a 2.88 metre wheelbase, sedan body and six-cylinder engine: its appeal reflected in the number sold — 1,754 models between 1936 and 1938.

The PV51-2 was mainly based on the Carioca with a similar streamlined look and, unlike its predecessor, was popular with all customers because of its spacious interior, economic performance and smooth ride. The PV52 range (1937-8) had a sedan body and over a thousand models appeared in the one year of manufacture.

PV53, with gas producer unit at rear

FV810, used as an ambulance

THE WAR AND 1940s

With the advent of World War II in 1939, Sweden looked to its manufacturing industries to assist in the war effort, Volvo becoming involved in the making of vehicles specifically for war use, and Volvo trucks were prepared for the army. In 1938 the PV53 made its début in Sweden, selling 1,204 models during the war, while the PV54 had 814 customers and the PV55 was purchased by 286 buyers.

During 1939 Volvo supplied the first producer gas units which allowed Sweden to conserve petrol stocks for military use; the gas units were run on wood and wood chips, generating a gas which was a good petrol substitute. Over 85,000 Swedish cars were kept mobile by producer gas units towed at the back of the cars and, although engine outputs were reduced, the invention allowed much needed petrol to be used for military purposes.

The PV56 was a successful Second World War car, selling over 1,320 models between 1938 and 1945, similar to earlier PV5 types in that it was 2.88 metres long, had six cylinders and a displacement of 3,670cc. The PV53-56 model dominated Volvo sales in the war years, being a spacious car with room for five, streamlined, and possessing many features in common with the PV36 or Carioca. One of the later designs in the PV5 range, the PV57ch, had a separate frame – unlike the former designs which had sedan bodies – and this latter model sold only 275 examples in the 1938 to 1945 period.

1938 heralded the start of the PV800 class of car, with the PV801-802 specifically made as a taxi, being 3.25 metres long and powered by an 84-86 h.p.engine. This eight seater taxi had three folding seats a top speed of 130 k.p.h. and, despite its seemingly huge size was easy to drive – even in the crowded city streets of Sweden. PV800 and PV810 cars had separate frames for the body and about 220 of these models were sold between 1938 and 1947.

During 1942 Volvo built five PV60 cars, but it was not until 1946 that serious production began on a car whose lines reflected the American streamline look, having good visibilty, plenty of space, and a three-speed gearbox, with overdrive offered as an optional extra. The 1946-1950 period saw over 3,000 examples of the PV60 on Swedish roads, with a sedan body type, 90 b.h.p., displacement of 3,670cc and a 2.85 metre wheelbase. The PV61 sold 500 models during the same period with the same technical specification as the PV60, but having a separate frame body type, rather than the sedan variety found in the PV60.

Following the Second World War, Volvo concentrated on marketing a car for civilian and general use, and also looked at new taxi models, since the TPV car in use by the Swedish Army in 1946 had a taxicab superstructure on an all wheel drive truck chassis, and the taxi section was shown to be very satisfactory. Consequently the PV820 models came on the

market, and soon the legendary Volvo taxi was seen throughout Sweden, the PV821 starting in 1948 with 200 models and the PV822 in 1944 to 1948 with 300 cars — being 3.25 metres long, powered by a six cylinder engine, with a displacement of 3,670cc and 90 b.h.p., both versions carrying seven or eight people. Considered to be practically indestructible, these sturdy machines were novel in that headlamps were mounted in the front mudguards, rather than on top of the mudguards as in earlier cars.

Such was the outstanding quality and reliability of the Volvo taxis that the company decided to interest the private car owner; therefore the PV823 and PV824 came on the market in 1947-48, similar in specification to the taxi, except for body type. So the 40s closed with Volvo cars proving an integral part of European markets, while the equally successful truck department manufactured about 5,000 models at the end of the 40s, of which one and a half thousand were exported.

PV60

13

VOLVO CARS IN THE 1950s

The first 444 at the 1944 exhibition

The 1950s saw several advances in car development, with England testing a turbine-powered car in 1950 and three years later two new tyre features appeared, as tubeless tyres were re-introduced and the radial ply tyre was put on the market.

For Volvo, the 50s began with the PV83 series and, from 1950 to 1957, over 4,000 PV831/832 cars were sold as taxis, with similar technical details as the PV821/822 types. During the same years, private motorists were given the chance to savour the delights of what was rapidly becoming a standard model, and Volvo introduced the PV833 and PV834, selling over 2,000, powered by a six cylinder engine and having a 3.55 metre wheelbase.

THE PV44 RANGE

At the 1944 Stockholm Volvo Exhibition, the world saw the Volvo PV444, which was to become the company's really long-run production car, since, when it was finally phased out in the mid-60s, over 440,000 examples had left the factory. The immense interest in this vehicle can be measured in a number of ways, such as the 6,000 modifications made on the PV444 between 1944 and 1958, and the fact that its basic design remained for twenty-one years, although continually improved.

14

PV444A

In 1944, the PV444A appeared as a four seater car, receiving power from a four cylinder engine, whose displacement was 1,414cc and the output was 40-44 h.p.: with a wheelbase of 2.60 metres, this model had the 2 - d Sedan body, which was unconventional being made of integral steel. The Design Department had started with a clean drawing board and an early idea had been for a rear wheel driven car with an eight cylinder two stroke radial engine mounted at the rear, but this was not generally accepted and the PV444 was the result.

The motoring public became fascinated by the PV444A series which sold over 1,200 between 1944 and 1950, the short stroke four cylinder engine of 40 h.p. making it economical to run, whilst independent front sus-pension and telescopic shock absorbers made for comfortable rides and good road holding: the new laminated windscreen was an added safety feature.

PV444

It is interesting to note that the war had resulted in a shortage of sheet metal, but that the price was comparatively low once sheet metal was again readily available after 1947.

International acclaim re-inforced Volvo's opinion that the PV444 was a remarkable car and a motor exhibition in Heidelberg awarded this marque the 'Concours d'Elégance'. The PV444B appeared in 1950, when 7,500 models were manufactured with the same technical speci-fications as the PV444A, while PV444C to H versions were introduced in the 1951 to 1955 span, all the same as their predecessors, with about 8,000 produced in this period, the earliest versions equipped with a flower vase attached to the ivory white and green dashboard to add some colour to the successful vehicle.

During 1950 the more powerful B4 engine, 44 h.p., was installed in models, while a new dashboard and starter motor switch in the ignition lock were added refinements. The PV444K's production run lasted two years, 1955-7, differing slightly from the earlier models of the A to H range in that the output h.p. was 51, as opposed to 44 h.p. Some measure of sales appeal was reflected in the 34,000 models on the road between 1955 and 1957, and this growing interest by drivers was forcing Volvo to update this highly successful car – in 1953 new bumper overriders were brought out, while the next year saw a one piece rear window, larger windscreens, better all-round vision and a bigger luggage compartment.

These modifications were apparent in the PV444L, whose c.c. displacement was now increased to 1,583 in 1957/8 with an output of 60 h.p., and whose sales were over 64,000 in this one year. By now the world had become informed about motoring achievements and events such as the Russian luxury ZIZ car that ceased production in 1955 being the last car to have an in-line eight cylinder engine. Volvo were, as usual, looking to the world market and their latest car was acclaimed by many experts as a reliable vehicle,

especially when Gunnar Andersson of the Volvo Competition Department became the 1958 European Rally Champion in a PV444.

Following the outstanding sales in the PV444 range, Volvo ventured further with the PV44 series, introducing the PV445A in 1953 and the PV445B in 1954/6, which sold over 1,000 in the period, having similar technical specifications as the PV444, except that the body was a separate frame, as opposed to the 2-d sedan type. The PV445D sold nearly 2,000 units in the years 1956 to 1958, while two subsequent cars, the PV445G and 445L only sold about 100 in 1958/60.

These same two years saw Volvo introduce the PV44511 and 44511 M which, in keeping with the 445L, had a 1,583 cc engine whose output was 60 h.p., compared to the 44 h.p. of earlier models.

With an eye to the expanding market, Volvo designed a commercial version of the PV444 in the form of the Duett, which appeared as a spacious station waggon/estate car, and whose versatility was reflected in widespread domestic use and also in its ideal rôle as an ambulance, offering good headroom in the patients' area.

The PV444 was probably the first main export model for Volvo, since the company went into the world market on quite a big scale, commencing with Scandinavian sales, and then moving to the rest of Europe and America. The sedan and pick up versions were selling well, as the PV445DH showed by the 6,400 manufactured between 1953 and 1956, being a reliable model with a 1,414 cc displacement and a 2.60 metre wheelbase. In subsequent pick up series, this trend was continued, with the PV445GL, that was available between 1956 and 1957, while the PV445LL of 1957 had over 800 examples made in that same year; and over 3,000 PV44506 pick ups produced in 1957-58, followed by the PV445 06 M (1958-60) with 60 h.p. engine and 2.60 metre wheelbase.

PV445

At this time, Volvo's constant interest in safety was in evidence as the company became the first in the world to equip car seat belts as standard components and, in 1959, three point seat belts came with Volvo cars. The outstanding reception for the P44 series continued in domestic and world markets and the company brought out the PV445 PH, with sedan, rather than pick up, body, seating two to five people, manufacturing nearly 1,200 in one year (1955), the PV445 GP (1956-7) attracting about 2,000 customers in its two years of production. In 1957 Volvo tried a sedan in the PV445 range, with 60 h.p., instead of 40 h.p., and about 1,000 of the PV445 GP range appeared in that year, reinforced by over 5,000 sedan body cars (1957-8) of the PV4407 version. During 1958 to 1960 there was the PV445 07M, which had a four cylinder engine and two to five seats.

The Duett (PV445/210) - commercial version of PV444

PV830

THE PV44 VAN

The ever popular PV44 versions were sweeping international markets as pick ups or saloon cars, so Volvo went further with the model, manufacturing over 1,300 PV445 D5 vans in 1953-6. The vans were powered by four cylinder engines with 1,583 cc displacement in the original model, while the PV445 G5 van (1956-7) had a 1,414 cc engine, as well as the 2.60 metre wheelbase which is seen in all the P44 vehicles.

During 1957 Volvo built over 500 PV445LS vans with a 60 h.p. output, and the years 1957-8 saw nearly 2,000 PV445 O5 vans with seating for two to five people. The last van in this group, the PV445 05 M, had a 1,583 cc engine and, like its predecessors, this 1958/60 van had four cylinders and seating for two to five people. The PV445 van era saw almost 4,000 vehicles manufactured for use by private owners and commercial organisations.

The years 1944 to 1960 were the time when Volvo shot to the top of the popularity tables with the PV44 range, selling over 225,000 cars, vans and pick ups in the P44 range alone during those sixteen years, in addition to other models, such as the PV83 and P1900, plus the PV554, which, not surprisingly, carried on from the P44 model.

VOLVO PV544 SERIES

In 1958 the PV444 became the PV544, whose specifications included a bigger rear window, a one piece windscreen and a redesigned interior. The attraction of this marque was demonstrated by its being made for seven years in a variety of models, the best selling type being the P544A, of which almost a hundred thousand were manufactured between 1958 and 1960, accommodating five people in a vehicle with 2.60 metre wheelbase, receiving power from a 1,583 cc four cylinder engine

Following on from the success of P544A in its early years, Volvo introduced the PV544B in 1960, of which about 35,000 were seen on the road, and the PV544C followed, complete with a larger engine - 1,788 cc, up-rated from the previous 1,583 cc variety - and between 1961 and 1962 around 38,000 examples of the PV544C car were manu-factured and, like the sub-sequent P544D (1962/3), were driven by four cylinder 1,778 cc engines. World interest in speed was aroused in the mid 60s by Donald Campbell's achievement of reaching a record 690 k.p.h. and, in the 1963/5 period, Volvo pressed on with the P544 range, introducing models E, F, and G - a total of approximately 65,000 cars in these years. Production of the PV544 series ceased in 1965 after an impressive run of some

PV544A

P210 MODELS

Whilst the PV544 was enjoying its success, Volvo introduced an interesting vehicle in the form of the P210 series, making about 12,000 in the P210A range during 1960/1, with a 1,583 cc engine for the P210A and P210B varieties, the 1,778 cc engine giving power to the P210C and P210D models, all of which had a 2.60 metre wheelbase and 75 h.p.

seven years in which the Volvo tradition for reliability and excellence was promoted in Swedish, European and world markets.

P120 series police cars

122-S engine view

P120 – 130 SERIES

In European competitions the PV544 had made its mark as a reliable and powerful machine suitable for the arduous rally scene or for domestic use and the introduction of the P120/130 series further demonstrated Volvo's genius for precision engineering and ability to create a tough car incorporating some impressive safety features. Unveiled in 1956 was the Volvo 121/122-S whose technical specifications and passenger comfort made it a keen rival for the more pretentious cars appearing elsewhere in the car market.

Swedish owners knew the 121/122-S as the Volvo Amazon and its roomy interior for five plus the shock absorbing steering wheel and padded fascia made this marque an immediate success. Some interesting design features added to the Amazon's popularity in Europe and abroad, especially in America where the 122-S was a success for a number of reasons, including the American

styling, its added height giving extra visibility in traffic and comfortable seats. For many Americans the Volvo 122-S was a rival to the Buick Special / 185 BHP in that new cars' prices were similar, but the Buick sported an automatic gearbox as opposed to the four forward manual gears of the 122-S and, in fact, had more interior space. The B10 engine gave power for the initial 121 cars, later changed to the B20, giving an output of 118 b.h.p. Talks took place between Volvo and a German motorcycle company concerning the name "Amazon", the Germans arguing that they were the first to use the title and, since this incident, all Volvo cars have numbers rather than names.

The magazine *Autosport* had, in 1962, a review of the Volvo 122 (which at the time cost only £1,294, including purchase tax) and gave some salient performance statistics, including the 94 m.p.h. maximum speed, 23 - 26 m.p.g.; and the magazine's summary of the 122 indicated that it was as economical as rival cars, while it had a good top speed and could be seen as an investment in

123

20

that it held its price in the second-hand market.

In 1959 the PV544, together with the PV121/122S, were the pioneers in the field by providing standard three point safety belts, while the robust body of the 121/122S could handle any accident bumps better than many rival cars. Early 121 models received power from B16 engines, changing later to the B20 variety and, in 1960/1, the P120 VD/HD sold almost 30,000 units, while a similar number of the P120 VE/HE range was sold in 1961/2, these cars exhibiting 1,778cc engines, as opposed to the 1,583cc model seen in the VD/HD designs.

The Volvo P120 VF/HF cars appeared in 1962/3 and proved to be four door sedans with five seats, 2.60 metre wheelbase and, in keeping with earlier designs, around 30,000 were manufactured in this

123GT

period, followed by the P120 VG/HG variety of which 2,600 were made in 1963/4. By now Gunnar Engellau was established with spectacular success as Volvo managing director and the company was clearly making a popular car in the P120 series, especially since the VK/HK (1964/5) again proved the strength of the 120 series' name, in that Volvo put out over 27,000 in one year, while over 3,000 VL/HL versions came off the production line in 1965/6, followed by the P120 VM/HM. These mid 60s models' seats were adjustable to give

21

lumbar support and, today, this original idea is a feature of Volvo cars and a further example of how the company endeavoured to provide top class passenger comfort as well as all round road safety and reliability. It was not only private motorists who appreciated the high quality cars of the 120 series; the Swedish police, for instance, employed 121/122S models, whose black and white livery made them easily recognisable.

Volvo wanted to attract as wide a range of customers as possible, so introduced a two door car whose four cylinder 1,778 cc engine, 2.66 metre wheelbase and room for five people was similar to the P120 range. This P130 vehicle came on the scene in the early 60s, remaining in production until 1970, alongside other designs such as the P120, 1800, PV544 and P210, all of which were manufactured during the 1960s. It is interesting to note that

sales in the first year of production (1961/2) were just over 10,000, while 1962/3 saw almost 30,000 P130 VB/HB cars coming off the line, with engines giving 75/90 h.p. The tremendous success of Volvo cars can be seen by the number made in the early 60s – almost 1,800 PV544D cars in 1962/3 and in the same period, 1,800 P210Cs and 2,720 P120 VF/HF vehicles were manufactured. The tradition of top quality P130 cars continued in the mid 60s when in the region of 200,000 P130 VE/HE, VF/HF and P130M vehicles were manufactured between 1964 and 1967.

Towards the close of the 60s Volvo decided to bring different engine capacities into the 130 series: up to 1968 all varieties had been driven by four cylinder 1,778 cc engines. The P130s range, however, was now equipped with a four cylinder 1,986 cc model (90/118 h.p.) in keeping with the P130T car (1969/70); the numbers produced for the S and T designs being 27,500 and about 20,000 respectively.

P130

220

THE FIRST VOLVO ESTATE CAR

Volvo had not always contructed saloon cars; in fact, the PV801 (1930s), PV821/831 (1940s) were used as taxis, the PV653, Duett and 245 as ambulances. The PV445 pick up was popular in the early 50s and, in order to cater for people wishing to carry loads too big for saloon cars, Volvo brought out the P220 in 1962 - an estate car (station wagon) coming in eight designs, to accommodate the small businessman or the family that wanted a vehicle for such uses as holidays or stowing ski gear. It is noteworthy that, in the 80s, Volvo still look after the sportsman; current cars in the 200 series, for instance, possessing an arm-rest in the rear seat, which may be lowered to accommodate long objects, such as skis, placed in the boot area and

lying on this arm-rest.

The P220 VA/HA was powered by a four cylinder 1,778 cc. engine and still retained the habitual 2.60 metre wheelbase, which was later extended to 2.62 metres for the 145 estate car and to 2.64 metres when the 245 estates came on the market in 1974. The distinctive lines of the 120/130 series could be sen in the radiator, bonnet and wing styling of the P220, with the grill divided in two sections, as in the 120 series, and this car proved popular for Swedish and foreign buyers. In 1962, the first year of prod-uction, about 1500 were made, while the P220 VB/HB and VD/HD (1962-4) series numbered over 16,000 and, in the VE/HE range, over 11,000 were manufactured in one year.

About this period of the mid 60s Volvo was enjoying success in the commercial vehicles sector, the System 8 range, for instance, appearing in 1965, with trucks such as the F82, F83, N84, F85 and so on. Their specifications included new ideas in engines and gearbox design. The F86 came on the market in 1965 with Volvo's first tiltable cab and proved most successful in Swedish and overseas markets. In the 1965/6 period over 15,000 P220 VH/HF estate cars came off the production line, featuring four cylinder engines with 85/100 h.p., and this estate retained a 1,778 cc. engine until 1968/9 when a 1,986 cc. version was introduced for the last year of production.

P1800

THE 1800 RANGE

The start of the 60s heralded a scientific era when speed and technical accomplishments were much in evidence as Gagarin became the first man into space. Volvo were already pleased with the 120/130 series of the 60s and realised that a fast sporty vehicle was needed to fill a niche in their production programme to cater for the driver who wanted the renowned Volvo qualities of car design and engineering, incorporated in a stylish, fast vehicle. The company had had thoughts on these lines some time earlier when, in 1956, the P1900 made its appearance as a convertible car with fibreglass body and a 1,414 cc. engine, but only a few of these had left the production line.

Anxious to create another highly saleable car, Volvo wisely looked abroad for guidelines in the sports car range. The first 6,000 P1800 vehicles were thus assembled by Jensen Motor Ltd. in England, production not moving to Sweden until 1963. The P1800 coupe was unveiled in Brussels, later being displayed at the New York International Car Show, causing considerable interest as its specifications included servo-

P1800

24

assisted hydraulic brakes, with drums at the rear and discs at the front. Jenson assembled and built the vehicle, Germany supplied the electrics and steering, the Frua body design came from Italy, and American back axles and dampers were employed. In the early 60s an English customer would have to pay £1,838 for a P1800, whose 1,780 cc. engine would give 100 b.h.p. at 5,500 r.p.m. and a maximum speed in excess of 100 m.p.h.

During the mid 60s British and American car journals examined the potential of the Volvo 1800, indicating that a maximum speed of almost 110 m.p.h. was possible, while some acceleration speeds were — 0-30 m.p.h.= 3.9 seconds, 0-60 m.p.h. = 11.9 seconds; the front 11" disc brakes and 9" drum brakes gave excellent braking, the front discs being well protected from dirt. The price for new Volvo P1800 cars was in the region of $5,400 for American models, in the early 70s, a U.K. dealer would want in the region of £2,640 for the 1800ES model.

Owners of 1800 cars may notice that the official title of the 1961/3 versions was 1800

1800S

VA/HA, whilst those built in Sweden after this date had the letter S added to their desig- nation, the 1800S VB/HB being the first model manufactured entirely in Sweden in 1963.

Powered by four cylinder 1,778 cc. engines, the 1800 series had varying h.p. outputs the first two models with 100 h.p., while the S VD/HD and S VE/HE both had 108 h.p. and, as international interest grew in this car, Volvo produced more; in 1965-8 manufacturing almost 1,200 1800S cars with 115 h.p. and the standard 2.45 metre wheelbase. To meet the needs of the motoring public and performance expected of their car, Volvo initially used

1800ES

the B18 engine, in 1961 moving to the B20 and, in 1969, using the impressive B20 together with electronically-controlled fuel injection. This latter type had the suffix E behind its title, the 1800ET of 1969-1970, for instance, giving an output of 130 h.p., the EU providing one of 135 h.p., as did the 1800EW, of which over 1,800 were constructed in 1971/2.

In the early 70s the P1800 was revised, Volvo providing a new look with features that included sleek lines and a large rear tail gate window. During 1971/3 over 8,000 1800 ESW/ESY two seaters were manufactured, equipped with 1,986 cc. engines giving an output of 135 h.p., while the wheelbase was still 2.45 metres as in earlier 1800 vehicles. There was a distinct similarity between the 1800ES and the Reliant Scimitar GTE car, particularly in the tail gate design and, although some research showed a maximum 112 m.p.h. for the Scimitar, compared to the 111 m.p.h. for the Volvo ES, the Swedish vehicle had, according to some road tests, better fuel consumption, giving an overall 20.6 m.p.g. (13.7 litres/100 km).

1800ES (right-hand drive)

142

THE 140/160 SERIES

144/142

The mid 60s saw Volvo altering their cars for domestic use as Sweden changed to driving on the right, and in 1966 the company launched the 144 whose safety features are legend and, at the same time, captured the interest of world and Swedish buyers. The 144 was awarded a 'Gold Medal' for contributions to car safety by Motormännens Riksforbund, the Swedish motoring organisation, and the country's *Teknikens Varld* referred to it as the 'Car of the Year'. For some time Volvo's name was linked to these reliable, rust free and endurant cars whose technical specifications were of the highest order and these, plus the 144's safety factors, augured well for this model and for subsequent designs. Thorough testing and arduous trials had brought about some safety devices which were standard on the 144 car, including the body designed to absorb impact at both front and rear, while the impressive braking system was constructed in such a way that, with only one circuit in use, eighty per cent of the braking potential was still available.

Initial research told Volvo that the 140 series would be successful as a larger car in two or four door versions, with room for five people. The first model, the 144M was produced in 1966 and, like the subsequent 144P, came with a 1,778 cc. engine, although the following six versions of the 144 gained power from the larger 1,986 cc. unit – the last model being the 144A in 1974. Two door, 142, cars sold well; in the final year of production, 1973/4, about 65,000 were manufactured with 2.62 metre wheelbases, catering for those owners who favoured two-door saloons, and offering eight models to choose from.

144 (left hand drive)

144 police cars

145

145

Following the breakthrough of
the P220M estate car (station
wagon) in the 60s, Volvo
realised the potential of a
similar vehicle based on the
proven features of the 144
range, so the year 1967 brought
about the introduction of the
145 estate car, whose distinctive lines and top class engineering made it an outstanding
success. Surprisingly, the 2.60
and 2.62 metre wheelbases
available were the same length
as those of the 144 saloon car,
but the spacious interior could
accommodate the needs of Swedish
and foreign drivers who used
145 estates for purposes such
as conveying holiday gear or
goods for business use.

The 145F had a 1,778 cc.
engine, whilst the 145 S/T/U/W/
Y and A versions possessed the
1,986 cc. unit whose h.p. ranged
from 90 to 135. In its first
seven years of production, the
number of 145 estate cars made
was in the region of 370,000,
many of which are in evidence
today, still proving as reliable
and popular as in 1967.

164

While in the process of making
144, 142 and 145 vehicles,
Volvo launched the 164 saloon
whose streamlined appearance,
leather upholstery and 2,978 cc
engine attracted many admirers;
the 164 being the first six
cylinder model to be exhibited
by Volvo since the PV60, dis-
continued in 1950. The radiator
grill of the 160 was most
distinctive, being less rectangular than 144 models, while
the headlamps were well
positioned in the curved front
wings. Available with four
doors, the 164 range provided
room for five people and 164S,
T and U types had engines with
a 145 h.p. output, whilst the
later 164 W/Y/A and B models
had 145-175 h.p. The elegant
lines of the 164 were enhanced
by the increase in wheelbase
length from the habitual 2.60/
2.62 metres of the 144 cars to
2.70/2.72 metres, this extra
length creating the appearance
of a sleek and roomy car with
one of the largest wheelbases
in the Volvo car range.

164

66GL

66 SERIES

In 1975 Volvo acquired the share majority of Volvo Car BV in Holland, thus increasing its resources and securing a strong position in the smaller and mid-range car market. Production of the Volvo 66 and 343 is based at Born in Holland and the CVT (continuously variable transmission) for the Volvo 66 is also manufactured at St. Truiden Belgium. The first model in the 66 series came off the production line in 1975; the 66E, a two door saloon car whose engine was considerably smaller than those in the previous vehicles – 1,108/1,789 as opposed to the well-known 1,778 and 1,986 cc. versions in the 144 range.

Built for the owner who had no need for the larger models,

about 20,000 66Es were made in the first year and, in 1976/8, the 66H and 66L cars came off the production line, again two door saloon cars, followed by the 66M in 1979. Some of the popularity of the 66 series can doubtlessly be attributed to its good performance and pleasant appearance – but the mid 70s was also a time when oil crises resulted in petrol rationing and increased fuel prices: the public needed a smaller car, like the 66, which combined traditional Volvo reliability with an economical fuel consumption. Volvo offered the 66E/H and L in estate car form, still retaining the saloon engine and 2.26 metre wheelbase and, in the three year period from 1975, over 28,000 of the 66 estate cars were made.

29

200 SERIES

THE SALOON CAR

Towards the close of the 1960s Volvo commenced work on an experimental car – the VESC (Volvo Experimental Safety Car) and vehicles from the 240/260 range feature many of the innovations and designs as a result of these experiments, making the range particularly acceptable in the USA where Ralph Nader was involved with road safety programmes. During 1974 the 242B car made its debut as a two-door car with a 1,986/2,127 cc. engine, followed by the 242E, 242H, L and M, all having 2.64 metre wheelbases. Volvo 244 cars included the 244B, manufactured in 1974/5, 244E (1975/6), H (1976/7), 244L (1977/8) and M (1978/9) and it should be pointed out that the designation alters slightly depending on the country in which it was sold; in the U.K., for instance, one can find the 244DL, 244GL, 244GLE and 244GLT

242

SPECIFICATIONS FOR 240/260 SALOON MODELS IN THE 1980s

Model	Engine	Steering	Fuel tank	Other notes
244DL	B21A 4 cyl. 2127 cc	Rack & pinion 21.3.1	60 litres /13.2 galls.	
244GLE	B21E 4 cyl. 2127 cc	As above	As above	Fuel injection Electric windows
244GLT	B23E 4 cyl. 2316 cc	17.2.1 Power assisted	As above	Acceleration 0–60 m.p.h. – 10 secs.
264GL/GLE	B28E V6.2,849 cc	17.2.1 Power assisted	As above	Overdrive, Sun roof, Fuel injection

244GLT

244DL engine compartment, dashboard, and general view

The 244DL, GL and GLE are suitable for conversion to operate on Liquefied Petroleum Gas (LPG), which means lower fuel costs, and the *Daily Telegraph* (February 1980) revealed that LPG was taxed at 18.4p. a gallon, only half as much as the tax on petrol. The mid 70s saw the advent of 244 series cars, whose four doors, engine output and reliability soon won huge orders for Volvo. In 1977 the A.A. road test report for the Volvo 244 spoke of the twin attributes of safety and durability, commenting, "It's no freak that Volvos have excellent reputation for durability... and Volvo are to be congratulated on achieving better fuel consumption with their latest cars." The 1977 price for a 244DL in the U.K. was £4,770 (GL £6,230) and, for this, the driver obtained a car whose name is legend for reliability and precision engineering. For many car owners, the campaign to buy British cars encouraged them to stick to domestic vehicles, but in 1977 Volvo was the largest single overseas buyer of British car components and parts, the total value at the time being over seventy million pounds and, in an attempt to influence the U.K. market, Volvo advertised the many British components found in Volvo cars, including tyres,

The standard accoutrements in the 244DL and other Volvo cars can make driving a pleasure: the driving seat is electrically heated automatically at temperatures below 14°C and front seats possess the Volvo lumbar support. Excellent heating and ventilation allows fourteen vents to direct the air where

244GL

automatic gearbox, brake pads, clutch plates, paint and shock absorbers.

New Volvo features for 1981 were the distinctive window surround, re-designed dashboard, the new front end and headlights, integral wraparound safety bumpers, which reduce the car's weight by some 12 kg. and its overall length by 10 cm., while a more shallow grille pleasantly blends with the wide rectangular headlamps.

needed, halogen headlights, day running lights, discus brakes all round, plus inertia reel seatbelts at the front and rear are all standard features, while a small 32'2" turning diameter makes for easy manoeuvring. It is little wonder that 240/260 Volvos are termed 'executive cars'.

264

ESTATE MODELS IN THE 240/260 SERIES

The 245B station wagon (estate car) made its début in 1974, followed by the 245E, H, L and M version in the 1975/9 period, all having a displacement of 1,986/2,127 cc., the move towards a more powerful engine resulting in the launch of the 265E station wagon in 1975, equipped with a 2,664cc. engine in the E, H, L and M marques, whilst from 1977, the 2,849 cc. version was available, this type's wheelbase measuring 2.65 metres, compared with the earlier 2.64 metres. The 1981 changes in design observed in the 244/264 series are in evidence, with the estate models still offering seating for five persons, 42 cubic feet of space behind the rear seat and over 70 cubic feet with the seat down.

245 station waggon

SPECIFICATIONS FOR 245/265 ESTATE CARS (STATION WAGONS)
IN THE 1980s

245DL   Powered by a 2.1 litre engine developing 107 b.h.p.; four speed manual gearbox or three speed automatic. Uusal Volvo standard equipment, such as halogen headlights and rear wiper/washer.

245GL   2.1 litre engine plus overdrive on the fourth gear for additional fuel economy, tinted glass, metallic paint and front spoiler.

245GLE   B21E fuel injection engine with 125 b.h.p., overdrive.

265GL   B28E engine, developed to give 155 h.p.

265GLE   B28E engine, all normal Volvo refinements, plus air conditioning, electric windows all round, and electrically operated door mirrors.

The international acclaim for the station wagon 245/265 model is, to an extent, helped by the versatility of such vehicles - useful for the small trader, while sportsmen enjoy the roomy interior and the 30 cwt. towing capacity, which, together with a 13'2" turning circle, encourages caravan owners to employ a 245/265 for hauling their trailers. The versatility of the 245 is high-lighted by a Canadian-built model, which completed a round-the-world trip in 1981 within 74 days, the Canadian driver covering 26,893 miles in a car which was standard, except for a sump shield and extra front lamps.

The 1976 Volvo was easily discernable on the road with its 20 watt 'day running lights' permanently switched-on, these lights being four times as powerful as the conventional side lights: these were espec-ially welcome by drivers in Sweden, Finland and the USA, where people tend to use lights in poor visibility more than in the U.K. Volvo was awarded the Swedish Automobile Association gold medal for the running lights and, in the 1980s, Volvo's rival Swedish car group introduced day running lights for its U.K. models, emphasising the safety aspect of such a feature.

It is the undoubted reliab-ility and ease of driving which attracted, not only, private motorists to the 240/160 range, but also police and ambulance services both abroad and in the

U.K.; Hampshire was the first police force in Britain to use foreign cars when, in 1965, a Volvo was included in the fleet; 1972 saw Cambridgeshire police acquire Volvos and, in recent years, Hampshire had over fifty Volvo cars for police work. It is interesting to recall that, in 1971, when Hampshire ordered a batch of Volvo cars, the Home Office intervened and suggested that the order be abandoned, which caused the Volvo company to complain that this decision was in breach of the E.F.T.A. trading agreement of which both Britain and Sweden were members and Hampshire police duly got their Volvos.

SAFETY AND RELIABILITY FEATURES IN THE 240/260 SERIES

Within the ambits of car safety and reliability, Volvo cars are generally accepted to lead the field, particularly in the 240/260 range, which incorporated such specifications from the VESC, Volvo's safety car, as the 'disappearing steering wheel', which moved into the dashboard in the event of a collision, and much other of the experience gained from the VESC project was later employed in the 240/260 series. The *Sunday Times* in June 1975 high-lighted seven salient aspects of Volvo's safety components, saying "Volvo was preoccupied with safety long before leg-islation caused the world's car makers to immerse themselves in the problem." The following factors were viewed by the newspaper as being worthy of

245 modified for ambulance duties

comment –

1.   Protected   passserger compartment.

2. Each of the six roof pillars can withstand the weight of the vehicle's 1.33 tons.

3. Dual circuit brakes system.

4. Halogen headlights, plus leadlamp wipers.

5. Impact bumpers.

6. Heated driver seat with excellent adjustments.

7. Steering column collapsible in four places.

The Volvo car of the 80s exhibits a triangle split dual circuit braking system, so that if one circuit should fail both front brakes and one rear will still function, while a Volvo 200 series will crumple and absorb much of an impact instead of transferring it to the passenger, the fuel tank being located away from the rear bumper, but outside the 'safety cage' surrounding occupants.

The rising cost of motoring demands a car which will be reliable and free of rust for a considerable time and, once again, independent sources testify to these features in Volvo cars – in the 70s a Chief Superintendant with Cambridge-shire Police stated that Volvo police cars proved reliable and, even after 125,000 miles, little trouble was experienced. *Car Magazine* 1978 surveyed a number of foreign and British cars with a view to examining rust appearance and, among its findings, the magazine listed twelve thorough rust preventing processes used by Volvo and refers to the car's extensive galvanisation, thick anti-chip paint, suggesting that the Volvo is built like an ocean liner and painted like one.

Naturally, Volvo themselves boast of these features, such as PVC underbody coating, PVC on sills and side panels, full underbody and inner cavity rust proofing, plus the fact that all parts of inaccessible closed sections are coated with zinc primer before welding. It is hardly surprising, therefore, that the Swedish Motor Vehicle Inspection Company recently gave Volvo the longest life

36

265GL

340 MODELS

expectancy off all cars on the Swedish market, including the 'Quality' executive cars of overseas origin in the same class. Perhaps twin fan belts, sealed cooling system and the larger-than-average battery contribute to the240/26C name of reliability, and a recent request by the company to *Motor Magazine* resulted in an engine compartment of a Volvo 244DL being swamped with water for ten minutes from a fire hose, drenching the battery, engine, distributor, etc. and, after a two minute interval following this, engulfing with high pressure water, the magazine said the engine sprang to life immediately. Finally, the share Volvo had in the executive car market in 1981/2 was at record levels, and the 200 series was the best selling executive car in June, 1981, with more bought than competitors from other motor groups.

The Volvo 343, like the 66, is constructed at St.Truiden in Belgium and, also in keeping with the 66, has the CVT (continuous variable transmission) providing a continuously variable ratio, giving the perfect ratio in keeping with the weight of the car and speed at which it is travelling 1976 was the date for the production of the 343E, a hatch

345DL

back with the 1,397 cc. engine. Following the 343E, Volvo introduced as a successor the H version, whilst 1977/9 saw the manufacture of 343L and 343M cars, nearly 70,000 of this latter type being made in 1978/9. The journal *What Car?* nominated the 343DL "Hatchback of the Year" in 1979 and recent developments include new wrap-around bumpers, GL door panels, together with a redesigned rear seat that includes the centre armrest on the GL version. The January, 1979, edition of *What Car?* further commented that the 343 handled well, had plenty of space and comfort, and was well equipped. The range of 340 series currently available in the United Kingdom is –

343DL 1.4 litre, 3-door hatchback
343DL 1.4 litre, 3-door hatchback, sunroof
343GL 1.4 litre, 3-door hatchback, metallic paint, tinted glass, spoiler, sunroof
345DL 1.4 litre, 5-door hatchback

345GL

343DL

345DL 1.4 litre, 5-door hatchback, sunroof
345GL 1.4 litre, 5-door hatchback, metallic paint, tinted glass, spoiler, sunroof, etc.

The five door models offer a 13.3 cubic ft. luggage compartment, (42 cubic ft. with rear seat folded down), plus all the normal Volvo standard safety and reliability qualities, such as servo-assisted, self-adjusting front disc brakes and a dual split braking system. The standard of seating comfort has been improved, details including new check-pattern upholstery

One of the latest 343GL

which is flame resistant, and a shallower grille set between bigger rectangular Halogen head lamps. Although most 343 owners are family men, happy with the spacious interior for luggage, some 343 drivers are determined to put the model through its paces – a new single driver record from Land's End to John O'Groats and back was created in 1980 by a rally driver in a standard 343, achieving an impressive time of 28 hours 57 minutes, beating the previous record by 2 hours 18 minutes and, in the same year, the European Rallycross title went to a works-prepared 343 driven by Swede, Per-Inge Walfridsson.

OTHER VOLVO CARS

Some Volvo cars never saw the production state, such as the Venus Bilo of the 30s, built by hand, and the Volvo City Taxi, especially designed for towns, incorporating a safety bar instead of seat belts. The P172 was intended to replace the P1800 as a car with a 200 k.p.h. top speed, while the P358 would have been powered by a V8 engine had it gone into production. The 1980s saw the VCC (Volvo Concept Car), whose specifications include an automatically adjusted seat, turbo-charged engine, display screen indicating such things as fuel consumption, while a front spoiler comes down automatically beneath the bumper when 70 k.p.h. is reached.

Some enthusiasts employ Volvos as 'customised' cars featuring unconventional engines suspension and interior designs.

Customised 121S, 1963

345

LV62 and LV40-45 trucks, 1929

VOLVO TRUCKS

"Swedish truck manufacture is renowned for high quality material, design and workmanship", so commences the instructions of the first Volvo truck built in 1928 and, over half a century later, this fame accounts for the international popularity of Volvo lorries. It is interesting to note that, in the early 80s, Volvo's leading truck markets in order of trucks purchased were - Great Britain, France, Sweden, U.S.A., Denmark, Holland, Belgium, Finland, Norway and Italy, but it should be noted that Volvos appear the world over in places, such as Australia and South America, where large scale local assembly of Volvo lorries is carried out. Following the success of Volvo cars, the end of the 70s saw Volvo trucks take a strong hold on North American, African and Asian markets and, in fact, over 90% of sales are to countries outside Sweden. Half of the production is put together in Göteborg, where test facilities and headquarters are found, while the other half of the production is assembled in a number of countries, including Scotland, Peru, Brazil, Belgium and Australia. The initial truck was the LV40 (1928), that received power from the same engine as the first cars, while subsequent marques included the LV60-63 (1929) and the LV66/67 trucks, which introduced the overhead valve engine in 1931; LV75 of 1933 and the LV94, LV190, making its déb18 in 1937 in which year three new series of heavy trucks appeared - LV180, LV190 and LV290, with payloads of up to 8 tons.

41

LV66 truck used by the Red Cross

In 1939, co-incident with the start of World War II, five new series were launched – the LV102, 110, 120, 125 and 130 – and, during the war, production concentrated on military vehicles although the latter part of 1944 emphasised Volvo's keen interest in the truck market, the company having made nine different models during the year, including their first diesel engine.

The LV150 series' successor was the L245, a new diesel truck that came on the market in 1949 with few outward improvements, but containing an

F86 at work in the U.K.

updated steering system and a five gear sychronised gearbox, while the following year was when Volvo introduced a new light truck in the form of the L340, whose six cylinder petrol engine developed 90 h.p. The advent of the 50s heralded a new breed of trucks as the L230 made its début as an all round truck with a payload capacity of five tons, while the L395 vehicle was equipped with a direct injection, in line, six cylinder diesel engine.

During 1953 the L385 appeared soon to be followed by the modified version, designated Volvo 'Viking', receiving power from a newly designed engine developing 115 h.p. The first servo-manufactured truck in the world with a turbo-compressor supercharged diesel engine entered the lorry market in 1954, entitled the L395, whose 185 h.p. output made it popular with a variety of operators since extra engine weight of only 3% resulted in 25% higher output, with the same fuel consumption, this later being improved to 50% higher output. In 1955 the L370 and L375 were brought out for light and medium-heavy transport and the L420 and L430 vehicles became the first to carry Volvo's V8 petrol engine designed for truck use; and 1957 brought power assisted steering and compressed air brakes to the heaviest lorries.

By now Volvo was rapidly becoming a force to be reckoned with on the truck scene: towards the end of the 70s the company's

F89 hauling timber

Moroccan plant started to produce trucks, while a totally new diesel engine developing 150 or 185 h.p. (Turbo) featured on the L495 whose specifications included dual curcuit braking system and a standard two-speed final drive.

The 1960s opened with the L4751 Tip Top with a tilting cab, followed by the L4851, L4951 Tip Top models, called this because of their tilting cabs which facilitated access to the engine: international acclaim from the 1964 Automobile Salon in Paris in the form of a Gold Medal for this design served to promote Volvo's good name. The company, about that time starting up assembly plant in Portugal and Iran, then opened new plant in Peru (1966)

Greece (1967) and Malaysia (1968), following the re-naming of trucks N84, F85, N86, N88, F82 and F83. The L4851 and 4951 were now designated F86 and F88 respectively, these vehicles boasting such components as eight-speed gearboxes plus new engines and the close of the 60s witnessed Volvo as the first in Europe with a torque multiplier for trucks, which doubled the tractive effort of the engine at the moment of starting.

1970 marked the inception of the F89 – a popular vehicle whose engine output was 330h.p. while the SR61 gearbox, appearing simultaneously, caught the market's eye in that

an overdrive on all eight speeds
gave a total of sixteen ratios,
thus permitting a good average
speed in long distance work.
New parts in the 1973 N7, N10
and N12 range encompassed a
variety of factors – new frames
plastic brake pipelines, plus
a safety cab, the tilting
bonnet made in fibreglass re-
inforced plastic.

The F406 – F613 series were
medium-heavy trucks with good
turning circles and the mid-70s
brought improved comfort for
drivers of F and N series
trucks, while the new N10 and
N12 were launched at the same
time, followed by the F10 and
F12 in 1977, these being suc-
cessors to F88 and F89 vehicles.
Some aspects of the F10 and F12
included an all-welded steel
cab, fire resistant interior
fittings, while the interior
noise level during acceleration
at 80 k.p.h. in top gear was
measured at 73dB(A), making for
a quiet drive. Available with
an extended cab for one or two

N7 negotiating a mountain bend

F4

bunks, the F10/F12 vehicles feature advanced air conditioning, air being fed into the cab through 24 outlets and most daily checkups (e.g. oil and washer fluid for windscreen and headlamps) can be done from outside the vehicle.

Built for short haul delivery work, the F4/F6 range includes seven basic models with gross weights ranging from 6.0 to 13.5 tons, driver comfort being ensured by lumbar support devices in the seat and a low noise level, while the cab can be tilted through 52°, allowing easy access to the engine. Announced in 1979, the F6 is similar to the F7, although lighter wheels and tyres are in evidence, and the 5.48 litre TD60B engine was never employed

on the U.K. truck scene and, compared to its predecessor, this engine displays a variety of improvements, such as modification to the injection system, resulting in less smoke and cleaner exhaust transmissions, while new valve seals reduce oil consumption, especially at low speeds.

The well-proven F85 and F86 lorries were replaced in 1978 by Volvo's F6S and F7 models, the F6S designed for short haul jobs, differing from its predecessor in aspects of safety and driver environment and powered by the TD60B engine, the F6S incorporating a cab lifting angle of 52°, while cab steps are of anti-slip design, illuminated when the door is opened.

F6 making a delivery

Replacing the F86, today's F7 is intended for heavy delivery work and is available in versions ranging from 16.5 to 24.5 tons, some details including rear view mirrors available with electric heating to combat condensation and ice, four independent braking systems — dual control footbrakes, trailer brake, parking brake and exhaust brake. The careful design of this lorry and its excellent safety and comfort aspects, contributed to its being voted 'Truck of the Year' this title being awarded because of certain features in the F7 as the advanced air conditioning available, letting the driver have any temperature level he wishes. An interesting aspect in the F7 development reflects the international background to Volvo, since Volvo's Scottish plant at Irvine makes a unique truck for Switzerland, where a maximum width regulation of 2.3 metres has provided work for Irvine where a modified F12

F6

47

F7 unloading

chassis is used in conjunction with the F7 cab, these vehicles being designated CH230's.

To bring in the 1980s, Volvo introduced the impressive F12 Globetrotter, equipped with the TD120F engine, developing an output of 385 h.p., coming with an Intercooler and a new twelve speed gearbox, together with a comfortable cab designed for long distance work, which can be specified with one or two bunks. The driver is able to make use of a fridge, table and equipment box, stainless steel sink unit and cooker — all valuable aids on long hauls — with internal headroom of not less than 197 cm. allows the driver to stand upright when, for instance, he may wish to change clothes. Windscreens and windows are tinted to reduce glare, whilst the crew seat turns through 180° and can be raked back 64° — all adding up to extra comfort on long continental journeys.

The fact that Volvo trucks are used in more than sixty countries reflects the high standard of testing carried out before a series is launched: the company's testing grounds at Hallered, near Gothenburg, have 15,000 kilometres of rugged test track and, in fact, the F10 and F12 lorries were given tests which equalled ten round trips to the moon before the public received the product in the late 70s.

F10s being loaded   F12 Globetrotter

F10 passing one of its early counterparts

LV102 rescue crane

FIRE VEHICLES

The illustrious Volvo name soon attracted the attention of fire authorities and Gothenburg, for example, acquired an LV81 and an LV94 fire appliance in 1939 and the LV102 rescue crane some five years later, the same brigade employing the LV192 for use as a turntable ladder in 1928. LV80/90 series fire vehicles could also be seen in Sweden during the 30s, often carrying a hydrant standpipe on the running board, whilst many airfield crashtenders were built on the F89 chassis.

The N720 appears in Norwegian and Swedish brigades as a pumping machine, while the well proven Volvo F12 followed on from the first generation of fire/crashtenders based on the F89 chassis, some features of

LV80 fire vehicle

the F12 being a climbing ability of better than 50% with the 6 x 6 chassis, high ground clearance of 310 mm. under the rear axle, 500 mm. under the transfer axle and 400 mm. under

LV94 fire engine with wheeled escape ladder

Laplander

the front axle. Continental air
ports have examples of the F12
in two versions, a 6 x 4 bogie
model and one of the 4 x 4
variety, both models available
with a crew cab accommodating
up top six fire personnel.

Smaller fire appliances
include the Laplander that
appeared in the mid 60s, together with the C202 appliance
which pumps 500 litres a minute
the Volvo B20A engine allowing
for a maximum speed of 115
k.p.h. The versatile C306
forest fire tenders' spec-

ifications include a 1,000 litre
tank for water or premixed
water/foam, a Ruberg H5 500
litres a minute pump, three
axles, two blue beacons, and
seating for six firemen;
available in left or right hand
drive versions, the C306 has a
top speed of 90 k.p.h., overall
length of 5.900 mm. and width
of 1.880 mm. A sister machine,
the C303, is particularly useful as a rapid intervention
fire appliance.

C303 at an oil fire

F12 airfield tender discharging foam

F89 at work

VOLVO BUSES

Right from the inauguration of the Volvo company, passenger vehicles were supplied to bus operators, initially as truck chassis with coackwork supplied by the customer, but later the B1 bus chassis came off the production line, available as a forward control or a normal ccntrol vehicle; the famous six cylinder petrol engine employed by the LV66 providing power for the B1, which made its début in 1934, although an option was offered in the form of a Hesselman engine, and the success of this first real bus chassis was reflected in a strong foreign interest, with five cf the first eighteen chassis acquired by a Brazilian client.

Subsequent models in the B1 series showed alterations in design, the length of chassis and new engines brought about the new titles of B10 and B20 chassis; the B40 bus stayed in production until 1944. Following the cessation of war, Volvo in-

B10

LV101

troduced their B510–B530 series the former being the forerunner of the more recent BB57 vehicle and public acclaim was directed at the B10's first Volvo diesel engine, the VDA. Trends in world passenger markets encouraged even more improvements in Volvo buses; the B530 was a new design featuring an interesting front axle, the model appearing as the first bus to have compressed air brakes, whilst the lower chassis floor level facilitated entry and exit.

The 1950s heralded the B615 series and the B635, renowned for its Volvo turbo-engine, at the time a novel and exciting component for the passenger transport world. Underfloor engines proved popular, not only in Sweden, but also with United Kingdom bus manufacturers, where the early 50s witnessed A E C, Leyland, Atkinson, Daimler and others making under floor engined single deck chassis, and so the B655 was Volvo's answer in 1951, when the first of a batch for Odense (Denmark) was delivered: in the early 80s all buses in Odense were Volvo, some capable of

B512

carrying over eighty passengers of whom fifty-three have to stand. Further improvements resulted in the B755 which was to serve as the model on which the B58 was based, over 10,000 examples of this latter bus being manufactured in 1976, its specifications including an engine positioned between the axles, so reducing the noise level, while the 1967 articulated bus (18 metres long) was based on a B58 chassis.

During the mid 60s, Volvo introduced their B57, followed by the B/BB57 in 1970, the former's engine positioned forwards of the front axle, allowing for one man operated service, while the latter had its engine placed above the front axle, thus reducing front overhang and easing driving in tight situations. The multifarious uses of these vehicles can be seen, not only in Sweden but elsewhere, where mobile libraries and outside broadcasting units are based on the dependable B57 and BB57 chassis. Engine placement for the B59 of 1971 is horizontally behind the rear axle and the low floor level, power steering and excellent suspension accounts for the widespread use of the model in, for example, Denmark, Sweden, Portugal, Australia and elsewhere.

An interesting development by Volvo in recent times is their offering turbo charged diesel engines, not only to the larger buses, but also to the smaller marques, the B6F serving as an instance of a forty seater powered by the six cylinder engine.

The B10R is Volvo's bus of the early 80s, bearing several similarities to the B59, including a good turning circle, low entry height and air springs, but also incorporating various neoteric specifications such as the sub-frame sections and improved braking. To allow for low entry heights, Volvo employ a special chassis design with separate sub-frame, the frame height measuring 513 mm. when the bus is equipped with 11/70 - 22.5 low profile tyres,

B655 in Denmark

and, interestingly, at the rear the sub-frame and the main frame are connected by a transverse strut, while at the front a flexible rubber mounting secures the sub-frame to the main frame. Designed with the driver in mind, the B10R features an impressive steering lock so that the vehicle can drive from a bus stop even if a vehicle is parked as close a 1.2 metres in front of the bus. The vehicle

whilst a pivotal battery box again allows the mechanic to easily handle that item. Together all these factors account for the B10R's popularity in Sweden, Belgium, Denmark, Holland, Switzerland, etc.

Volvo has employed mid engined buses from 1951, the recent B10M chassis proving its worth in a number of ways — whether empty or full, the mid underfloor engine of the B10M

B57 in Finland

is powered by the THD 100D six cylinder direct injection diesel, accelerating from 0 – 40 k.p.h. in 16 seconds with the derated engine version.

Repairs to the B10R are helped by the easy access to the engine, reached by means of a raised rear panel and every cylinder is equipped with a separate cylinder head. Battery cables are fused, so eliminating fires starting from there,

ensures the centre of gravity is always in the middle, while the engine compartment is entirely separate from the passenger area, so leaving the interior of the bus completely free for maximum use of floor space. The mid-underfloor horizontally-placed engine encourages a variety of uses, such as the B10M articulated bus, the tourist coach, and a city bus capable of carrying large doors anywhere along its sides, while a choice of eight

B10M with Van Hool bodywork

different gearboxes adds to the vehicle's versatility. The driving force is a horizontal in-line six cylinder turbo charged diesel engine placed exactly in the centre of the vehicle, with power output as high as 178 kW (ISO 2534), and B10M buses display a powered air brakes system or three separate circuits, one for each of the front and rear axles and the third for the parking brake Instances of U.K. operators possessing B10 coaches include Wallace Arnold and Western SMT (Scotland) and it is worth noting that a B10M won the coveted Coach of the Year Award in Brighton in 1981.

B10M articulated bus in Greece

A popular coach in U.K. and world markets, the B58 Volvo single decker, is available as the B58-56 with a 222" wheelbase or the B58-61, featuring a 240" wheelbase. The long wheelbase, wide spread axles, together with a mid-mounted engine, ensure a stable ride; the Volvo six cylinder, four stroke diesel engine having direct interjection combustion chambers located in piston crowns. Among U.K. varieties of the B58 series, a model with Wadham Stringer body is framed throughout with a 45 mm. welded box section forming a multiple rig structure providing added strength in the event of the vehicle rolling over, and Duple Dominant bodies also appear on the B58 chassis, the Dominant 2, 3 and 4 bodies exhibiting a

detachable lower front panel, thus facilitating quick replacement after damage.

Perhaps one of the more surprising ventures by Volvo is the Ailsa double deck underframe with Alexander one example of a coachbuilder providing bodywork for this double decker which contains all welded rectangular box sections with strong cross members. Powered by Volvo's TD70H type six cylinder four stroke diesel engine, the Ailsa features a flat lower saloon throughout the entire length of the vehicle, a rear mounted fuel tank accommodating 200 litres (45 gallons) and the handbrake is very safe in that total braking effect remains even should the ordinary air pressure fail totally. Some operators with Ailsa Mark III double deckers include Manchester PTE, West

B58 with Plaxton bodywork

Ailsa with Alexander bodywork

Midlands, and Strathclyde PTE, who received about thirty buses in 1981/2. Recent surveys show an intensification of Volvo buses on U.K. roads during the 1980s.

B58 with Duple Dominant II coachwork

B10M articulated bus with Hess coachwork

2654 tractor at work

AGRICULTURAL VEHICLES

AND OTHER PRODUCTS

Any title on Volvo would be un-
fair to the group if it failed
to outline products other than
cars, trucks and buses, as

B5350 articulated dump truck

4300 earth mover

Volvo Penta industrial and marine engines provide power for boats and generate electric power, while Volvo Flygmotor builds jet engines for Viggen fighter plans and, through subsidiaries, Volvo markets such products as gear for camping and ice hockey.

Volvo BM is one of the principal manufacturers of agricultural and forestry machines and earth-moving equipment, with plants at Eskilstung, Arvika, Hällsberg, Braås, and Hallby, the range of Volvo tractors including model 2654 with power take off coupling, the 2250, 2254, and the 2204 developing 56 h.p. Volvo earthmovers include the 4300 and the BM4400 which is in the 11 tonne class, powered by a turbodiesel engine whose bucket capacity is 1.9m³ (2.5yd.), whilst the smaller B4200 weighs 5,700 kg (12,570 lbs) and has a 49kW DIN engine. Other products include the BM5350 articulated dump truck, the BM4500 14 ton loader, these designs having improved considerably from the days of the first Swedish tractor built by Volvo in 1913 and the 1924 motorgrader vehicle (both before the company moved into the motor car market). Similarly, the advances in car and truck design have come a long way since the inception of Volvo cars in the 20s, when the 'Jakob' car first left the production line.

1924 motorgrader

A history of the cars produced by Volvo in Sweden
and at other factories around the world since 1926.
Substantial sections on Volvo trucks, fire engines,
buses and other vehicles.
95 photographs

IAN HENRY PUBLICATIONS Ltd.
38 Parkstone Avenue, Hornchurch, Essex, RM11 3LW

86025 838 6

£4.25
Net in UK only